S. W. Sanderson

The Stockton and Visalia Railroad Co., Petitioner

vs. the Common Council of the City of Stockton, Respondent

S. W. Sanderson

The Stockton and Visalia Railroad Co., Petitioner
vs. the Common Council of the City of Stockton, Respondent

ISBN/EAN: 9783744746465

Printed in Europe, USA, Canada, Australia, Japan

Cover: Foto ©Suzi / pixelio.de

More available books at **www.hansebooks.com**

No.

IN THE

Supreme Court

OF THE

STATE OF CALIFORNIA.

THE STOCKTON & VISALIA RAILROAD CO.
Petitioner,

vs.

The Common Council of the City of Stockton,
Respondent.

Brief on behalf of the Southern Pacific Railroad Company, filed by leave of the Court granted upon the consent of Counsel of record for both parties.

S. W. SANDERSON,
FOR S. P. R. R. CO.

SACRAMENTO :
H. S. CROCKER & CO., PRINTERS, 42 AND 44 J STREET.
1870.

No. ....

In the Supreme Court

OF THE

STATE OF CALIFORNIA.

THE STOCKTON AND VISALIA RAIL-
ROAD COMPANY,

                Petitioner,

vs.

THE COMMON COUNCIL OF THE CITY
OF STOCKTON,

                Respondent.

Brief on behalf of the Southern Pacific Railroad Company, filed by leave of the Court granted upon the consent of Counsel of record for both parties.

The limited time which has been allowed for the preparation of this brief, renders it impossible to do more than touch upon what appear to be the principal points in the case. I shall therefore not undertake to answer in detail the very able briefs which have been filed on behalf of the Respondent; nor shall I undertake to review cases—for two reasons—first, I have not the time, and second, that duty has already been performed by other Counsel.

The question, which the case presents, is whether legislation which authorizes counties and cities to aid in the construction of railroads, which are to pass through their borders, by donations, in the form of county or city bonds, to the corporations proposing to construct them, is valid under the Constitution of this State.

Those who claim that such legislation is unconstitutional, do so upon the following grounds:

First. That such legislation is not an exercise of the power of eminent domain, because it takes the property of the citizen " without just compensation," which compensation is made a condition, by the Constitution, to the exercise of that power.

Second. That such legislation can be upheld under no legislative power unless it be the power of taxation.

Third. That such legislation cannot be sustained as an exercise of the taxing power, because that power is a power " to take from the citizen a certain proportion of his property to be expended for *public* purposes," while the legislation in question takes a portion of his property to be expended for a *private* purpose.

Fourth. That whether a given tax is for a public or private use, is a *judicial* and not a *legislative* question.

Fifth. That, in addition to the foregoing considerations, there are certain express provisions of the Constitution to which this legislation is repugnant, viz: The clause which provides that "no person shall be deprived of life, liberty or property without due process of law"—the clause in the Bill of Rights, which enumerates the inalienable rights of persons in relation to life, liberty, property, safety and happiness—the clause in relation to the formation of incorporations, other than municipal, under general laws and not by special Acts—the clause in relation to the organization of cities and incorporated villages, and restricting their power of taxation, assessments, etc., so as to prevent abuses—the clause providing that the credit of the State shall not be loaned to or in aid of any individual, association or corporation—and lastly, the clause which requires that taxation shall be equal and uniform.

I think the foregoing is a fair statement of the positions which have been assumed by the enemies of this legislation, and the reasons by which their alleged soundness has been attempted to be maintained. The soundness of some of these propositions is admitted, and that of others denied.

First. It is admitted that such legislation is not an exercise of the power of eminent domain.

Second. It is admitted that it can be sustained only upon the ground that it is an exercise of the power of taxation.

Third. It is admitted for the sake of the argument, but denied as an abstract proposition, that the power of taxation is a power to take a percentage of the property of the citizen for *public* purposes only.

It is denied, First: That such legislation takes a percentage of the property of the citizen for *private* purposes.

Second. It is denied that whether a given tax is for a public or private purpose is a judicial, not a legislative question, and the contrary affirmed.

Third. It is denied that either of the clauses of the Constitution specially referred to above, prohibits such legislation.

As it is not deemed necessary to dwell at length upon the question whether this kind of legislation is repugnant to the several express clauses of the

Constitution specially referred to above, they will be first considered.

I.

The idea that this legislation is repugnant to that clause of the Constitution which provides that no person shall be deprived of life, liberty or property. without due process of law, is founded upon an utter misapprehension of the object which that provision was intended to secure. It is to be found in all American Constitutions. It was borrowed, or inherited, from *Magna Charta.* It is the provision of that instrument by which the Barons of England extorted from King John a royal pledge that the right of trial by jury should remain forever inviolate. The language of *Magna Charta* is: " *Nec super eum ibimus, nec super mittimus, nisi per legale judicium parium sucrum,* VEL PER LEGEM TERRÆ "—(neither will we pass upon him, or condemn him, but by the lawful judgment of his peers, *or by the law of the land*). Lord Coke says that these latter words, " *per legem terræ* " (by the law of the land) mean *by due process of law;* that is, without due presentment or indictment, and being brought in to answer thereto, by due process of the common law. " So that," says Judge Story, " this clause in effect affirms the right of trial according to the process and proceedings of the common law." (2 Story on the

Constitution, §1789.) Instead of the phrase, "by the law of the land," which was used in *Magna Charta*, the phrase employed by Lord Coke in defining its meaning has been substituted in American Constitutions. The clause relates to judicial and not legislative functions. The idea that this clause of *Magna Charta* had anything to do with the exercise of the taxing power, would have astonished the Kings and Barons of England. Taxes were not then, nor are they now, assessed, apportioned, or collected by or according to common law methods, but by Acts passed by the Commons of Great Britain in Parliament assembled, who first fixed the amount to be raised and then prescribed the ways and means by which it was to be collected. (1 Blackstone, 308.)

But concede, for the sake of the argument, that this clause of the Constitution is broad enough and was intended to include the exercise of the power of taxation, what pretense is there for saying that this tax, if collected, will be collected *without due process of law?* It will have been levied, apportioned, and collected according to express laws passed by the law-making power. The property of the citizen will have been taken, then, according to law; that is to say, by due process of law. When the citizen has been deprived of his life, liberty, or property by the operation of,

and according to. a valid law, how can it be said
that he has been so deprived "without due process of *law?*"

(a)

If there be any repugnancy between this
legislation and that clause of the Bill of Rights
which enumerates the inalienable rights of persons, it must be because it proposes to take the
property of A and give it to B, or in other words,
to tax the citizen for a private purpose (as claimed
by the opponents of this legislation), which I
deny, and will endeavor to establish when I come
to consider what is a *public use,* and by whom the
question of *public* or *private* use is to be determined. If, as I claim, this legislation is a Constitutional exercise of the taxing power, it is obvious that it cannot be repugnant to the Bill of
Rights, for the acquisition, possession and enjoy-
ment of property there mentioned does not include exemption from taxation.

(b)

It is not perceived what bearing the clause of
the Constitution, in relation to the formation of
corporations, other than municipal, has upon the
question now before the Court. The language of
that clause is as follows : " Corporations may be
formed under general laws, but shall not be created by special Act, except for municipal purpo-

ses." There can be no doubt about the object, and the only object intended to be secured by this provision. It was considered that the creation of corporations, other than municipal, by special Acts, would be troublesome and mischievous, for such had proved to be the case in older States. It was therefore provided that there should be but one rule for their creation, which should be declared in a general law. It was further considered, however, that for obvious reasons, a general rule would be impracticable in respect to the creation of municipal corporations. Hence they were excepted from this limitation and left to stand, in relation to the Legislature, upon precisely the same ground upon which they would have stood had no such clause been inserted in the Constitution—upon precisely the same ground upon which they now stand in States where no such constitutional restriction exists. The whole purpose and effect of this clause has been, and is, to prohibit the creation of any corporations, other than municipal, by special statute. It spends its whole force upon the former class of corporations. It places no restrictions upon the power of the Legislature in respect to the latter class, but on the contrary leaves them where they were before—to be created by general or special laws in the discretion of the Legislature, without any restriction what-

ever, either as to the mode of their creation, or
the extent or character of the franchises and
powers to be granted to them. If there be any
constitutional reason why municipal corporations
cannot be authorized to aid in the construction
of a railroad under the provisions of the statute
now before the Court, it must be sought for in
some other place. The idea that the word "municipal," which is obviously used solely for the
purpose of *classification*, was used to limit the
powers to be conferred by the Legislature upon
that class of corporations, with all due deference
to the opinion of the Attorney General and those
who think with him, is simply absurd. There is
nothing in the Constitution of this State which
provides what powers shall or shall not be conferred upon municipal corporations. Such a
clause in a Constituton would be most anomalous,
and it has been wisely left to the Legislature to
confer such powers upon them as circumstances
may seem to demand at the time of their creation. "So far as municipal corporations are in-
vested with subordinate legislative powers for local purposes, they are mere instrumentalities of
the State for the convenient administration of the
Government, and their powers are under the entire control of the Legislature; they may be qualified, enlarged, restricted, or withdrawn at its discretion." (*Grogan* vs. *San Francisco*, 8 Cal. 613.)

2

(c)

The only clause of the Constitution which has even a cognate relation, in this connection, to the question involved in this case, is the thirty-seventh section of the fourth Article, which reads as follows :

"It shall be the duty of the Legislature to provide for the organization of cities and incorporated villages, and to restrict their power of taxation, assessment, borrowing money, contracting debts, and loaning their credit, so as to prevent abuses in assessments and in contracting debts by such municipal corporations."

This obviously belongs to that class of constitutional provisions which are *advisory* or *directory*. Instead of restricting the powers to be conferred upon municipal corporations, in the matters of taxation, assessments, borrowing money, contracting debts, and loaning their credit, it assumes that such powers are indispensable to corporations of that class, and that they must and will be conferred by the Legislature, and simply enjoins upon the Legislature the duty of guarding the exercise of such powers in such a manner as to prevent abuses, thus leaving the whole matter entirely in the discretion of the Legislature. As to the purposes or objects for which the powers enumerated may be exercised, not a word is said, but they, too, are left to the discretion of the Legislature. In all respects municipal corpora-

tions are left in the hands of the Legislature
with the mere injunction to see that they do not
abuse their powers, but leaving that body to determine for itself what will and what will not
amount to an abuse. Finally, instead of prohibiting what the statute now before the Court per-
mits, this clause of the Constitution directly
sanctions the act, if in the opinion of the Legislature it does not amount to an abuse. That the
act does not amount to an abuse in the judgment of that body, the statute now before the
Court is conclusive evidence.

(d)

That the tenth section of the eleventh
Article of the Constitution which provides that
"The credit of the State shall not, in any manner, be given or loaned to, or in aid of any individual, association, or corporation; nor shall the
State directly or indirectly become a stockholder
in any association or corporation," does not prohibit this legislation, has been demonstrated by
one who once sat upon the Bench of this Court;
therefore no more need be done than to refer this
Court to what he said. In *Pattison* vs. *The Board
of Supervisors of Yuba County*, 13 Cal. 175, it was
argued, as it has been in this case, that a restriction upon the State was also a restriction upon
each political subdivision of the State, and there-
2*

fore that the Legislature could not enable counties or cities to do what it was itself prohibited
from doing in behalf of the State. Replying to
this argument Judge Baldwin said :

" But the radical error of the argument is, this provision
only applies to the *State* as a corporation—as a political
sovereign represented by her law-making power. As such
corporation, or sovereign being, she has no subdivisions, for
sovereignty is not divisible. She may have political subdivisions—that is, she may permit a portion of her powers
of government to be exercised by local agents, who, of
course, are her subordinates. But politically considered,
geographical or political departments are no more the
State or a part of the State, than a man's land, or his
agent is a part of himself. The intent of this clause of the
Constitution is plain enough ; it was designed as a check
on legislation, and such legislation *as might create a charge
upon the property of the entire State.* But it is not only
unwarranted by the words of the Constitution to suppose
that counties were included in this inhibition, but it might
well have been foreseen that the provision would prove
extremely embarrassing. .* * * The general powers
of Government being vested in the Legislature, the power
to pass this law must be conceded, unless some constitutional restriction is imposed. *We see no restriction in this
case.* The fact that the State could not take stock in this
road does not show that the Legislature could not authorize the county of Yuba to take stock ; for the reason that
the Constitution says the State shall not subscribe, and
does not say that the county of Yuba shall not. *The
restriction goes no further than the language carries it.* It
comprehends the particular act and party interdicted—
none other." (Page 183)

To hold that this interdiction upon the State
is also an interdiction upon counties and cities, is
to put words in the Constitution which its fram-

ers omitted, and to overturn a well settled rule of Constitutional and statutory construction—*Expressio unius exclusio alterius est.*

That such is the proper construction may be further illustrated by reference to another and cognate provision of the Constitution, viz: The eighth Article, which restricts the creation of an indebtedness exceeding the sum of three hundred thousand dollars, except in certain cases there specified. If the reasoning of the adversaries of this legislation proves that counties and cities cannot loan their credit, in aid of a corporation, because the State cannot, it must inevitably follow that this restriction upon State indebtedness also includes counties and cities, and that the indebtedness of the State, counties and cities, combined, can never be allowed to exceed the sum of three hundred thousand dollars, except in the cases otherwise provided for, without a violation of the Constitution. Speaking of this provision, in the case of *Pattison* vs. *The Board of Supervisors of Yuba county*, already referred to, Justice Baldwin said:

"It is not only unwarranted by the words of the Constitution to suppose that counties were included in this inhibition, but it might well have been foreseen that the provision would prove extremely embarrassing, if it did not entirely stop the operations of those local governments. All of them, or nearly all, we believe, have been obliged to go in debt to support themselves; and, besides, the restriction would be wholly impracticable, for how ascertain from time to time, whether the aggregate of this indebtedness passed the limit, and when, or whether, by payments or otherwise, returned within it again? For the question of the validity of any contract or debt would depend upon the general balance of State and county debts or credits. Many cases have come before this court involving the validity of these debts, but the point has never before been taken; *and we think there is not enough plausibility in it to justify a more detailed exposition of its fallacy."*

To overturn this construction would block the wheels of government; yet, it is respectfully submitted, that this Court cannot give, to the clause prohibiting the State from loaning her credit, the construction for which the Attorney General contends, without doing so.

The Word Municipal Not an Interdiction upon the Power.

As being german to the foregoing, it is deemed best, at this stage of the argument, to examine the proposition advanced by the Attorney General, that the word " municipal," by itself considered, contains an interdiction upon the power under consideration.

It is said that the power to build railroads or to aid in their construction by the exercise of the local power of taxation, is no legitimate part of a municipal government. A complete answer to this argument is found in the circumstance that the Constitution nowhere defines a municipal government—nowhere provides what kind, or how much power a municipal government shall have, but leaves the whole matter to the Legislature. But assuming, as the argument undertakes to show, that the word "municipal" operates in some way as a restriction upon the power of such governments, and creates in them an incapacity to take certain powers, it remains to determine whether the power under consideration belongs to that class.

The same point was made in the case of *The City of Aurora* vs. *West* (9 Ind. 74), and I cannot do better than quote what the Supreme Court of Indiana said in reply:

" The question therefore presents itself, can such power be given to a city? Of the policy of conferring it, we have said all that becomes us to say, in *The City of Lafayette* vs. *Cox*, 5 Ind. R. 38, to which we refer. Of the capacity to confer it, we have not heretofore expressed an opinion. That is now the question. We have seen that no express Constitutional provision stands in the way of granting such power to a city, as we hold that the prohibition in the Constitution upon the Legislature to create a State debt, does not prohibit that body from authorizing cities to create debts. This is our construction of the language of the Constitution. But it is insisted that the power is not a legitimate part of the authority of a municipal corporation—that it is outside of the purpose for which such corporations are created—and that this is a sufficient reason for holding them incompetent to receive a grant of such power. But is not this begging the very question to be decided? For what precise purpose are municipal corporations created ? How much power, and no more nor no less, is embraced by the idea of a municipal corporation? We have not been satisfactorily enlight-

ened on this point. If the Legislature can confer a little
legislative power upon a city for local objects, can it not
confer a greater amount for the same objects? It would
hardly be said that cities were created simply to establish
and enforce police regulations — to maintain order
amongst the citizens. By common custom they establish
sanitary regulations, rules governing markets, etc.; and on
what principle do they exercise these powers? They go
further. They construct streets, side-walks, bridges, etc.,
within their limits. They do more. They build wharves
to accommodate their trade and commerce, coming to them
from a distance; they construct water works — going for
the purpose miles beyond corporate limits. They construct
works for lighting, etc. These, and other like powers,
though not existing in every one, yet, we believe, all concede, may be conferred upon municipal corporations as
legitimate, as Constitutional, though in their exercise the
citizens are not severally equally benefited in proportion
to taxes paid. Now if a city may build wharves, or take
stock in companies created to build them, to foster commerce—may take stock in companies chartered to furnish
the people with water, light, etc.—why, as a question of
power, may it not take stock in companies for the making
of highways to facilitate the bringing in of bread, and
meat and fuel to the citizens? Are not these of nearly as
much importance to them as water, light, etc ? And are
not such works, in a special manner, locally advantageous
to the city? And when the citizens of a place have seen
fit to ask, and the Legislature to grant such power, and
the citizens have subsequently, in the prescribed mode,
exercised it, no Constitutional provision forbidding, a
court, whose province is simply to decide what the law is,
not what it should be, cannot annul such exercise of
power. How much local benefit must an improvement
confer to bring it within the spirit of a local one? If a
city may build a wharf to accommodate its commerce, may
it not, also, a depot? May it not build the track of a
road through its corporate limits? *May it not, then, put in
that amount of stock or bonds to pay* the company the sum
the depot and track would cost?"   *   *   *

The further position, taken by counsel in this case, to the effect that conceding the power to cities of aiding, by the exercise of the taxing power, the construction of such local improvements as expend their benefits upon their citizens, and no one else, still the power does not extend to improvements which may also benefit other persons, did not escape the eye of the Court in the above case. Speaking to this point the Court further said:

"It is true, the water-works may benefit nobody but the citizens of the city, while the railroad may benefit the surrounding country, to some extent, at the same time it confers a great local benefit on the city— one, perhaps, greater than the water works. But, where such is the case, should the city be deprived of the right to benefit itself locally, because it cannot do so without also benefiting others? And if the argument is a good one, that cities are necessarily incapable of aiding any improvement that may extend beyond the corporate limits, will it not apply with equal force to States? May it not be said that a State is created to govern within its territorial limits; and, hence, that it is unconstitutional for it to aid any work extending beyond those limits? That Indiana, therefore. could not aid in the construction of the *Wabash and Erie Canal*, because it extended into Ohio?— That she could not, with the consent of Ohio, construct that portion of the *Whitewater Canal*, lying in that State, because it was without her territorial limits?—That South Carolina could not aid in the construction of a railroad to *Memphis*, in *Tennessee*, or to *New Orleans*, in *Louisiana?* But is this the doctrine? *A State can do what its Constitution does not, by positive provision, or reasonable implication, prohibit.* The United States, and city corporations, can do only what their Constitutions permit. If the Consti-

3

tution of the United States expressly authorized the Gov
ernment to construct, with the consent of the States, road
within their limits, would there be any doubt of their
power to do so?   If a State, then, can construct, by per-
mission—if *South Carolina* can, with the consent of *Tennessee*, construct a road in that State—cannot a city of a
State be authorized by the State to take stock in a road
extending beyond her corporate limits?   We think the
proposition may be asserted, that one Government may
act within the territorial limits of another with the consent
of the latter."

This reasoning, which has received the approval
of this Court, in the case already cited, I submit,
leaves nothing to be said in answer to the proposition that there is some undefined prohibitory
force inherent in a municipal corporation which
incapacitates it to receive the power in question,
if the Corporation asks it and the Legislature sees
proper to confer it.   If by taxation the city' of
San Francisco can bring in the waters of Tahoe, a
distance of two hundred and fifty miles, and make
them tributary to the necessities of her citizens,
which no stickler for a strict construction of municipal power can deny, with any show of reason,
may she not, instead of incurring the whole cost,
donate a part of it to the corporation which proposes to do the same thing?   If, in the judgment
of her citizens, a bridge across the Bay of San
Francisco would facilitate her trade, travel and
commerce, does any one doubt her power to build
it by taxation, if the Legislature grants the pow-

er? And, if she may, can she not, instead of building it, contribute to the means of a corporation which proposes to build it? The mere word "municipal" can no more limit the powers of a municipal government than it can limit the necessities and wants of its people. The former must keep pace with the latter, and the latter will be found to keep pace with invention and discovery, or human progress in all the departments of social and material life.

(e)

It has been so often held by this Court that the clause of the Constitution which directs that "taxation shall be equal and uniform throughout the State," applies only to impositions upon property for the purposes of revenue (merely exacting, even in such cases, equality and uniformity in assessments), and has no application whatever to taxes levied for other purposes, that to dwell upon this point is considered a waste of time. (1 Cal. 232; 2 Cal. 590; 4 Cal. 46; 12 Cal. 76; 13 Cal. 343.)

My conclusion upon the points thus far considered is, that there is nothing in the express or implied limitations of the Constitution which prohibits this kind of legislation, unless such legislation can be shown to be a misuse or abuse of the taxing power, by itself considered, for the

reason, as alleged by its enemies, that its purpose
and object is *private* and not *public*, which is the
only question in the case about which there can
be any rational controversy. All other points
are but make-weights.

II.

The Attorney General has quoted in his brief
various definitions of the power of taxation. So
far as they go they are doubtless unobjectionable.
They are doubtless comprehensive enough to answer all the calls of ordinary occasions, but it is
manifest that they are but blind guides in the
present case, for to say that it is a power which
can be exercised only to subserve a public purpose, or use, and there stop, is to give but a very
vague and unsatisfactory idea of its nature. The
reason is unsatisfied and at once inquires: "But
what is a public use?" And until that question
is answered, no very clear conception of the nature and extent of the taxing power can be
reached. The words "public use" occur in that
clause of the Constitution which puts a limitation upon the exercise of the power of eminent
domain —"Nor shall private property be taken
for *public use* without just compensation." Under
the head of eminent domain unnumbered cases
are to be found in which the term "public use"
has received definitions at the hands of both Leg-

islative and Judicial bodies, not only in an abstract way, but by examples. It has been defined by this court to be "a use which concerns the whole community, as distinguished from a particular individual or a particular number of individuals. It is not necessary, however, that each and every individual member of society should have the same degree of interest in this use or be personally, or directly affected by it, in order to make it public."   *   *   *   "If the use   *   *

*   be to satisfy a great public want or public exingency, it is a public use.   *   *

*   But no definition is given of public uses" (in the Constitution). "We have seen however that this public use need not be a use general or common to all the people of the State alike. It may be a use in which but a small portion of the public will be directly benefited, as a street in a town, a bridge or a railroad, necessarily local in its benefits and advantages, though it must be of such a character as that the general public may, if they choose, avail themselves of it. It has also been seen that it is not essential to meet the requirement, that the use or benefit should be exclusively for the people of the State or even a portion of those people. This was held in a case in New York, and we can see no answer to the proposition that the people of California have no right to complain that the people of Ore-

gon are also benefited by a public improvement, or that such improvement would be any the less a public use in California because it was also useful elsewhere." (*Gilmer* vs. *Lime Point*, 18 Cal. 251.)

Said this Court, on another occasion: "Whether a way be public or private does not depend upon the number of people who use it, but upon the fact that every one may lawfully use it who has occasion." (*Sherman* vs. *Buick*, 32 Cal. 252.)

It is true these definitions were given in cases involving the power of eminent domain, but whatever can be held to be a public use, in respect to the power of eminent domain, must be held to be a public use in repect to the power of taxation. For the two powers, so far as the purpose for which they can be exercised is concerned are, by definition, identical. Either may be exercised for a public purpose, and neither can be exercised for a private purpose. The only difference between them lies in the circumstance that one takes the specific property, and the whole of it, of a particular individual, and the other takes equal parts of the property of all the members of the community. To take the entire specific property of one person, and not of the other members of the community, would be unequal, unjust and oppressive; hence the restriction upon the act which requires that just compensation shall be made. But where an equal part of the property of each member of the body politic is taken, there is, theoretically at least, no inequality, no injustice, no oppression; hence there is no such restriction or limitation upon the taxing power. Said Chief Justice Marshall, in *McCullough* vs. *The State of Maryland* (4 Wheaton, 316), "the power of taxation is a power to destroy—it has no limit except the will of the sovereign by whom it is exercised."

Railroads a Public Use.

It is too late to doubt the public character of railroads. It has been definitively settled with scarcely a dissenting voice, by both Legislative and Judicial action, as well as the common consent of all civilized nations, that railroads are *improved highways*, which afford vastly increased facilities for travel and transportation, and, as such, have become so necessary to the convenience and accommodation of the public as to justify Legislative bodies, throughout the civilized world, in putting them, in relation to the taxing power, upon a level with ordinary highways, or wagon-roads, which, as every one knows, are constructed and kept in repair at the public expense through the exercise of the taxing power.

Said Bacon: "There be three things which make a nation great and prosperous: a fertile soil, busy workshops, and easy conveyance of men and things from one place to another." Said Raynal: "Let us travel over all the countries of the earth, and wherever we shall find no facility of passing from a city to a town, or from a village to a hamlet, there we may pronounce the people to be barbarians."

In *Sherman* vs. *Buich* (32 Cal. 252), this Court has said:

"To lay out and establish roads or highways is exclusively within the power and control of the Government. To do so is one of its most important and onerous duties. * * * Whether a given road will subserve the public need or convenience is a question for the Government alone to determine."

Accordingly in the performance of this duty, the Government may determine what kind, or character, of road is demanded by the public need or convenience; and may accordingly provide that an ordinary mud road, or mud turnpike, or a plank, or a McAdam road, or a railroad shall be built, according to its opinion of what the public exigencies may require. Governments have the same power to build railroads and operate them by taxation that they have to build ordinary roads, or other ways for transportation and travel. It was by the exercise of this

power of taxation that New York constructed
and still owns and operates the Erie and other
canals, aggregating in length eight hundred and
eighty-six miles. That Pennsylvania constructed
a canal from Columbia to Hollidaysburg, a distance of one hundred and eighty-one miles—a
canal from Johnstown to Pittsburg, a distance of
one hundred and one miles—a double track railroad from Philadelphia to Harrisburg, a distance
of eighty-one miles—a railroad between Johnstown and Hollidaysburg, a distance of thirty-
seven miles; all of which were sold by the State to
the Pennsylvania Central Railroad Co. in 1858
for seven and a half millions of dollars; also five
other canals forming a continuous line from the
Juniata river to the New York State line, a distance of one hundred and sixty miles; also the
Delaware division of the State canals from Bris-
tol to Easton, a distance of sixty miles, which
were also sold by the State to the Sudbury and
Erie Railroad Company, in 1858, for the sum of
three and a half millions of dollars.

It was also by the exercise of this power of
taxation that the State of Maryland constructed
the Chesapeake and Ohio Canal, some two hundred miles in length, at a cost of five millions of
dollars; also the Chesapeake and Delaware Canal,
and also the Susquehanna Canal.

4

By virtue of the same power Ohio constructed the Ohio Canal, from the Ohio river to Lake Erie, a distance of three hundred and seven miles, and other canals too numerous to mention, aggregating a total length of eight hundred and twenty-seven miles, costing over fifteen millions of dollars.

To the same use has the power of taxation been put by the State of Michigan in the commencement and partial completion of the Michigan Central Railroad and the Michigan Southern Railroad, both having been sold to private parties before their completion.

The same is true of Illinois. In 1839 that State built and opened as a State road the Sangamon and Morgan Railroad, extending from Springfield to Naples, a distance of fifty-six miles; also a part of the Chicago, Alton and St. Louis Railroad; also the Illinois and Michigan Canal, extending from Chicago to La Salle, a distance of one hundred miles.

Under the same power the Kingdom of Belgium has constructed and still owns and operates all the railroads in her borders, aggregating about four hundred miles in length; and other continental governments have built railroads and either operate them directly or lease them for a term of years to private parties.

And, lastly, it was by the exercise of this power that the Government of the United States has done, what otherwise might not have been done during the present century, secured the completion of the greatest work of the age—the Pacific Railroad, by which the East and West have been made to come together.

It has been said, however, that it may be admitted that Governments may construct railroads and operate them through the exercise of the taxing power; and that such railroads, while they remain in the ownership of the Government, are public uses, but that roads not constructed directly by the Government, or which, as in Pennsylvania and other States, have been so constructed and afterwards sold to individuals or corporations, are not, or have ceased to be public uses in the sense of the taxing power.

The utter fallacy of this view should be apparent to every one. It ignores a legal relation and a legal maxim with which every lawyer is familiar—that the title to a thing may be in one, and the right to use it in another, and *qui facit per alium, facit per se.* In constructing, managing and controlling roads of any kind or character, the Government may act by itself or by agents. If in the former mode, the road is constructed by levying a tax upon the property of persons resi-

ding in the road district through which it is to
pass; and after it has been constructed, it is to be
maintained and kept in repair by a further annual
tax to be paid by the tax-payers of the district.
If the latter mode is adopted, and in later times
it has generally been the case, in respect to all
improved highways, a franchise or right to construct the road is granted by the Government to
private individuals or corporations, *not for their
use or benefit*, but for the use and 'benefit of the
public. Such individuals or corporations become
the agents, or instrumentalities, of the Government for the purpose of performing a duty to the
public which the Government would otherwise
have to perform through itself. To compensate
these agents for their services in constructing
these roads, the Government delegates to them a
part of its sovereignty, and vests them with
power to collect such tolls as the Government
may determine to be adequate compensation.
Roads of this latter character are not less public
highways than the former, nor are they any the
less constructed for *public* and not *private* use.
Both are the acts of the Government, acting under
the power of taxation. The only difference is
one of mode and manner. In the one case the
public is taxed directly, and at stated seasons, to
enable the State to construct and maintain the
road; in the other, the public is taxed only when

they use the road, in the form of tolls. To this latter class, railroads belong, and in no respect touching the power of the Government to construct, or to cause them to be constructed, do they differ. They are constructed and maintained by the Government through the agency of corporations which are compensated for doing so by the franchise which enables them to demand and receive fares and freights. Every one has the same right to use them which he has to use a mud turnpike. It is true that he cannot use them in the same way, but this difference is not due to the object for which they are constructed, but to the nature of such roads, which does not admit of such a mode of use.

From the introduction of railroads to the present time, the Legislatures, it is believed, of every State in the Union, have delegated the power of eminent domain, which can be exercised only to subserve some public necessity, to railroad corporations, and the Courts have held, without a dissenting voice, that such legislation is constitutional. As that power can be exercised only to subserve a public use, we have the combined testimony of all the legislative and judicial bodies in the country, that railroads are highways, and that their construction is therefore an object for which the Government may provide—may either construct them directly, or cause them to be constructed, by granting a franchise to that effect to private parties, with a right to collect tolls (which is a form of taxation) by way of compensation, the same as in the case of toll-bridges, ferries, turnpikes and plank roads.

Said Chancellor Walworth, in *Beekman* vs. *Saratoga and Schenectady Railroad Co.* (3 Paige, 75):

"The privilege of making a road and taking tolls thereon is a franchise, as much as the establishment of a ferry or a public wharf, and taking tolls for the use of the same. *The public have an interest in the use of the railroad*, and the owners may be prosecuted for damages sustained, if they should refuse to transport an individual, or his property, without any reasonable excuse, upon being paid the usual rate of fare."

Again in *Bloodgood* vs. *M. and H. Railroad Co.* (18 Wend. 16), speaking upon the same subject, he said:

"It might as well be objected that a canal, made by an incorporated company, was not a *public* improvement, because each individual could not navigate it with a canal boat, or travel thereon with a steam engine, or that a turnpike road was of no public utility, because each citizen could not conveniently transport produce and passengers thereon with his wagon and horses."

Said Senator Edwards, in the same case :

"It is entirely immaterial who constructs the road, or defrays the expense of the construction. The *object* for which it is constructed must determine the nature of the grant, *whether for public or private use.* What object have the Legislature in view, in authorizing this Company to construct the road in question on the plaintiff's land? It was not the private emolument the Company was to receive for the use of the road. *For such a purpose the right would never have been conferred.* The Legislature, *who are constituted the judges* of the expediency of taking private property for public use, came to the conclusion that the *public required the use of a railroad* between the cities of Albany and Schenectady. *It deemed it expedient* to construct it, *at the public expense,* and adopted the policy of having a company construct it, at its own expense and risk, having the money refunded by way of tolls or fares from the individuals who should travel upon it. * * * Because the Legislature permitted the Company to *remunerate itself for the expense of constructing the road,* from those who should travel upon it, *its private character is not established ; it does not destroy the public nature of the road, or convert it from a public to a private use.*"

In the case of the *Lexington and Ohio Railroad Company* vs. *Applegate* (8 Dana, 295), the Supreme Court of Kentucky said:

" Public roads, of *all sorts,* may be constructed wherever the sovereign shall be pleased to have them ; and if the public choose to avail itself of the capital and liberal spirit of select persons for insuring the construction of an important highway, the persons who may agree to thus appropriate their own funds, may surely be permitted to enjoy, as some equivalent for the expenditure, the profits of tolls prescribed by law for using the road, and may be authorized to construct and preserve it by all the means which the Commonwealth could constitutionally employ. The sovereign will can be effecuated only by the instrumentality of agents. And in the case just supposed, the private association should be deemed the agent of the public, *although, as to its conventional privileges and profits, it may be only a private corporation ;* and the road also should be considered, in the popular sense, *a public highway.* In 4 East, second edition, page 21, it was held that though the lord of the fee was entitled to the profits arising from the use of an established road, yet it was a public highway —*'le haut chemin du Roy.'* When the Legislature incorporates an association of private persons for the purpose of making a turnpike road, *or a railroad,* the *public welfare* should be *presumed* to be the *legislative* object of the enactment; and though the interest of the corporators be *private* and *exclusive,* yet the construction of the road should be deemed to have been authorized for the *public good,* AS THE CHIEF AND PRIMARY OBJECT; and the Act of incorporation, and the privileges granted to the corporators, should be considered only *as means* for effecting the *public end,* and as *secondary* and *incidental only.* And, to accomplish such an end by such means, the sovereign power may undoubtedly, as we think, exert, through such an instrumentality, all the constitutional authority which it might employ for the effectuation of a similar object *by any other agency, or in any other mode.* The railroad is applied to *'public use,'* though the profits are applied to *private use.*"

In the case of *Raleigh and Gaston Railroad Company* vs. *Davis* (2 Dev. & Batt. 468), the Supreme Court of North Carolina said:

" Upon the supposition that the Legislature may take the property to the public use, it is next said, that this taking is not legitimate, *because the property is bestowed on private persons.* It is true that this is a private corporation ; its outlays and emoluments being individual property ; *but it is constituted to effect public benefit* by means of a *road,* and that is *publici juris.* In earlier times, there seems to have been a necessity upon Governments, or at least it was settled policy with them, *to effect everything of this sort by the direct and sole agency of the Government.* The highways were made by the public, and the use was accordingly *free* to the public. The Government assumed exclusive direction as well as authority, as if they chose to be seen and felt in everything, and would avoid even a remote connection between *private interest* and *public institutions.* An immense and beneficial revolution has been brought about in modern times, by engaging individual enterprise, industry and economy, in the execution of public works of internal improvement. The general management has been left to individuals whose private interests prompt them to conduct it beneficially to the public; *but it is not entirely confided to them.* From the nature of their undertaking and the character of the work, they are under sufficient responsibilities to insure the construction and preservation of the work, *which is the great object of the Government. The public interest and control are neither destroyed nor suspended.* The control continues as far as it is consistent with the interests granted, and in all cases as far as may be necessary to the public use. *The road is a highway,* although the tolls may be private property.   *   *   *   As to the corporation, it is a franchise, like a ferry or any other. *As to the public, it is a highway,* and in *the strictest sense, publici juris.*"

So in the case of *Osborn* vs. *The United States Bank* (9 Wheaton, 860). The question was whether the Bank was a public or private institution. If the latter, its business could be taxed by the States, but if the former, its business could not be taxed by the States. It was argued that the Bank was a *private* institution, because four-fifths of its capital stock was owned by private individuals, and it was engaged in part in the banking business on *private* account from which *private profit* and gain were made. But Chief Justice Marshall said:

5

" The Bank is not considered as a private corporation
whose principal object is individual trade and individual
profit; but as a *public* corporation, created for *public* and
national purposes. That the mere business of banking is,
in its own nature, a private business, and may be carried
on by individuals and companies, *having no political* connection with the Government, is admitted; but the Bank
is not such an individual or company. *It was not created
for its own sake or for private purposes.* It has never been
supposed that Congress could create such a corporation·
* * * It is not an instrument which the Government
found ready made, and has supposed to be adapted to its
purposes, but one which was created in the form in which
it now appears, *for national purposes only.* It is, undoubtedly, capable of transacting *private* as well as *public* business. While it is the great instrument by which the fiscal
operations of the Government are effected, *it is also trading with individuals for its own advantage.* The appellant
endeavors to distinguish between this trade and its *agency
for the public,* between its banking operations and those
qualities which it possesses in common with every corporation such as individuality, immortality, etc."

The Chief Justice then proceeded to show at
length, the fallacy of the attempted distinction,
and ruled that the circumstance *that private individuals were interested in the operations of the bank,
and were employing its franchises for the purposes of
private trade and private profit,* DID NOT DETRACT AT
ALL FROM THE PUBLIC CHARACTER OF THAT INSTITUTION.

In a late case in Pennsylvania (*Foster* vs. *Fow-
ler & Co.* 61 P. S. R. 27) the question was
whether a mechanic's lien was valid in law against
the property of a corporation chartered for the
purpose of introducing water into certain towns

in that State, which property was essential to the operations of the corporation; and that question turned upon the further question whether the corporation was to be considered as of a *public* or *private* character. In discussing that question the Court said:

"Most people acquainted at all with corporate action, understand that corporations, other than municipal, which are *purely* public, naturally divide into public and private corporations; that is, into those that are *agencies* of the public *directly* affecting it, and those which only affect it *indirectly*, by adding to its prosperity in developing its natural resources, or improving its mental or moral qualities. Of the former, are corporations for the building of *bridges, turnpike roads, railroads, canals,* and the like. *The public is directly interested in the results to be produced by such corporations, in the facilities afforded to travel and the movements of trade and commerce.* * * * This direct benefit to, and accommodation to the public clearly distinguish this class of corporations from the second class, viz: *private* corporations, or those in which the *public is but indirectly* interested, such as mining and manufacturing, or coal and iron companies, etc., or libraries, literary societies, schools, and the like. Whether they progress or cease, the public is not directly affected. * * * It is something, also, that the Legislature regarded this as a public corporation by giving it the power of eminent domain. Still, if it were not essentially so in its nature, the power would not make it so. *The power itself would fall.* Private property cannot be taken on any terms by legislative authority for private purposes. This is effectually prohibited by the tenth section of Article first of the Constitution of the United States. But we think the power was properly conceded to the purpose in this case, *it being public in its* nature and design."

This division of corporations into purely public, purely private, and mixed, that is to say, partly public and partly private, has been recognized and declared by this Court. In the case of the *Miners' Ditch Company* vs. *Zellerbach*, 37 Cal., 577, Chief Justice Sawyer says :

" There are several classes of corporations, such as public municipal corporations, the leading object of which is to promote the public interest; corporations *technically private*, but yet of a *quasi public character*, having in view some great public enterprise, *in which the public interests are directly involved to such an extent as to justify conferring upon them important Government powers*, such as an exercise of the right of eminent domain ; of this class are railroad, turnpike and canal companies; and corporations *strictly private*, the direct object of which is to promote private interests, and in which the public has no concern, except the indirect benefits resulting from the promotion of travel, and the development of the general resources of the country."

These cases furnish a conclusive answer to the theory of the Attorney General, and those who think with him, that railroad corporations are *purely private* corporations, and stand in all respects, except the mere right to be a corporation, upon the level of natural persons. If such be the case, it may be pertinently asked whence comes the power, continually exercised by legislative bodies, of regulating fares and freights ; of putting a price upon services rendered by such corporations? No such power is ever exercised over the business of *purely* private corporations, formed for trading and commercial purposes. Such an interference in their case would be an unjustifiable meddling with the natural rights of persons which are possessed by them in the same degree that such rights are possessed by individuals.

It is undoubtedly true, that some text writers, in classifying corporations, have placed railroad, canal, turnpike and bridge corporations in the class of private corporations. It is also undoubtedly true that the Courts sometime speak of them as belonging to that class, but *writers and Judges thus speaking must be understood in a qualified sense.* Chief Justice Marshall and the Supreme Courts of North Carolina, Kentucky, Pennsylvania and California have not overlooked in the cases above referred to, the circumstance that there is between the two classes of corporations —*purely public* and *purely private*—a middle class, which possesses some of the characteristics of each; and in respect to them have drawn a very obvious and just distinction, and one, too, which puts them, in relation to the powers of eminent domain and taxation, upon the same level with corporations classed as *purely public.* When Judge Cooley and the Attorney General declare railroads to be upon the same level with purely trading or commercial corporations, they ignore or fail to note this most obvious distinction, and therein lies the principal vice in their argument.

When they assert that railroads are made for the benefits of private individuals, as their chief and primary object, they mistake the *incident* for the *principal*, and attribute to the Legislature a motive directly opposite to that which, as we have seen, must be *presumed*. If no *direct* benefit flows from a given corporation to the *public*, it must undoubtedly be classed as *private;* and such a corporation cannot be endowed with the power of eminent domain, nor can the public be taxed to aid it. But if a direct *benefit* flows from it to the *public*, then it must be classed as public *whenever its relation* to the Government is considered; and this quality is unaffected by the circumstance that a benefit may also flow from it to private individuals. If its object and design be public, *in part only*, that circumstance is sufficient to give the Legislature the power to help it, to foster it, on the one hand, and to regulate and control it on the other. The moment that it appears that the public has a *direct* interest in the objects and purposes of the corporation, that moment the corporation becomes a thing of *public concern*, about which it is the duty of the Government to interest itself, to aid it, if there be occasion, in the judgment of the Legislature, and in any event, to so regulate and control it as to prevent abuses. When Governor Haight, in his published letters upon this subject, admitted that

" railroads are a potent civilizing agency and confer *great benefit* upon every State in which they
are constructed," he felt and recognized their
public character, and could not have more im-
pressively recommended them to the fostering
care of the State. When Judge Cooley admitted,
in his recent decision, that the same object can
be *public* in one sense and *private* in another, he
overturned his own position and completely re-
futed his own argument. If the object be public *in any sense* the Government may regard it in
that sense, and deal with it in that sense. If the
object and purpose of a corporation be to subserve both a public and private end, who shall
dictate to the Government in which character it
shall be regarded. By what right does Judge
Cooley say to the State of Michigan, "in one
sense railroads are of a public character, but in
another sense they are of a private character;
they are of a great public benefit, for they add
immensely to the facilities of travel and transportation, but they are also of a great private
benefit, for they put money in the purses of private individuals, and hence in dealing with them
you must close your eyes to their public use and
open them only to their private use?" Most
lame and impotent conclusion ! A most glaring
non sequitur! The reverse is the true deduction.
How much more in consonance with reason is the

conclusion drawn from the same premises by the Chief Justice of Maine: "We apprehend that the question of constitutionality does not, in *judicial consideration*, depend on the *proportion which the public interest bears to private interest."* (*Spring* vs. *Russell*, 7 Maine, 245.)

The idea advanced by Judge Cooley, that railroads, if owned and operated by the Government, are public uses, but if owned and operated by private individuals or corporations, are not, is not founded in reason. The fallacy of the distinction is apparent. It may be exposed by reference to the status of ordinary or unimproved highways, the title to which is vested in the owners of the adjoining lands; but no one has yet affirmed that for that reason such highways are private uses. When Judge Cooley admits that the State of Michigan did not violate the Constitution in undertaking the construction of the Michigan Central and Michigan Southern Railroads, that is to say, did constitutionally exercise the power of taxation in constructing them, and yet, in the same breath, affirms that those roads became mere private uses the moment that the title to them passed to the vendees of the State, he falls into the error of confounding the means by which the end is accomplished with the end itself. Judge Cooley, and those who think with him, will admit that the canals and railroads which were constructed, and for a time, operated, by the State of Pensylvania, were during that time public uses for which the power of taxation could be constitutionally exercised. If, while in that condition, they were public uses, it must have been because they responded to the exigencies and necessities of the public; did they do less when they had passed from the ownership of the State to that of her vendees? On the contrary, was not their relation to the public precisely what it had been before the transfer? Before the transfer, the public enjoyed the use of them upon payment to the State of certain fares and freights, or tolls. After the transfer they enjoyed the same rights, upon the payment of fares and freights to the corporations. There was, then, no change in the *end* for which they had been constructed, but only a change in the *instrumentalities* by which the end was to be attained. The interest of the public in them remained wholly unaffected by the transfer, and, whether the public have a direct interest being the acknowledged test whether a use be public or private, it must inevitably follow, that if they were public uses before the transfer, they remained, for the same reason, public uses after the transfer had taken place.

Nothing can be more illogical than to argue that because the Government wisely sees proper to avail itself of private capital in the performance of its acknowledged obligation to the people to provide them with the most improved ways of travel and transportation, the interest of the public in such ways has become in anywise diminished thereby, or that such ways have become any the less of public concern, or less subservient to the convenience and necessities of the people. Nor is it less illogical to argue that the Government cannot use the private capital which thus comes to its aid if the latter proves inadequate to the undertaking. It would seem to be incontrovertible that if the Government may supply all the capital required for the construction of a given railroad, it may do less by supplying a part only. Suppose a railroad is demanded by the public necessities, between two given points, no one contends in the absence of constitutional restrictions that the Government cannot build it by the exercise of the taxing power. If private capital offers to build it, experience teaches that it would be good policy on the part of the Government to accept the offer. But suppose private capital hesitates—is willing to assume three-fourths of the cost, but is unwilling to assume it all, who, in view of the premises, is prepared to maintain that the Government may contribute the whole but cannot the part? Such an absurd position might deprive the places in question of all railroad facilities until by slower processes their wealth and population assumes proportions which will embolden private capital to take upon itself the whole burden. The effect of such doctrines, if they are sound, will be most disastrous.

They will stay the development of the country for half a century, or entail upon the Government the necessity of inaugurating a system of internal improvements solely at the public expense, which, as all experience teaches, is to be avoided whenever private capital is willing to assume the burden. Instead of such a course, the true policy is to aid and encourage private capital, as this legislation was designed to do, in assuming these burdens of the Government. A contrary course, as declared by Mill in his great work on Liberty, might lead to most disastrous consequences: "If the roads, the railways, the banks, the insurance companies, the great joint stock companies, the universities, and the public charities, were all of them branches of the Government—if the employees of all these different enterprises were appointed and paid by the Government, and looked to the Government for every rise in life—not all the freedom of the press, and popular Constitutions of the Legislature, would make this or any other country free otherwise than in name."

Public Use a Legislative Question.

The power exercised by American Courts of annulling legislative Acts on the ground of their supposed repugnancy to some provision of the Constitution is anomalous. The power, it is believed, exists nowhere except in the United States; but even under our form of Government there are a variety of questions upon which the judgment sometimes of the law-making power, and sometimes of the executive, is necessarily conclusive. The Courts, for example, cannot determine what the *letter* of the Constitution is— they can only read and interpret. (*Luther* vs. *Borden*, 7 How. U. S. R. 1.) They cannot determine whether a political contingency has arisen which alone justifies special action on the part of the Legislature, or whether a state of war or insurrection exists. (*People* vs, *Pacheco*, 27 Cal. 175; *Martin* vs. *Mott*, 12 Wheaton, 19.) They cannot determine what Acts are mischievous and shall be prohibited as criminal (*ex-parte* Smith and Keating, 38 Cal. 707); and generally all questions of necessity, expediency, and policy, are beyond the reach of the Judiciary. What will subserve the interests of the public, on the score of legislation, rests with the Legislature. The general power to look after the wants, necessities, convenience, and general welfare and prosperity of the people, is vested in the Legislature, and, as incident to its exercise, that body must judge of the exigency and the means to meet it. What concerns the public rests upon their judgment. What is a public use under the power of eminent domain, and the power of taxation, is a legislative and not a judical question.

In the case of the *Commonwealth* vs. *Bruel* (4 Pick. 460), it was claimed that the Legislature had no power to obstruct a navigable stream by granting the right to a private individual to bridge it, *because the bridge was not needed by the public.* The Court said:

"But it is said that this grant was made upon the petition and for the sole benefit of an individual, and was not needed for the accommodation of the public. It is doubt- less true, that the leading motive of the defendant in erect- ing the bridge was private profit. And so almost all other enterprises, many of which have resulted in great public improvements, have originated in motives of private gain. It is also true, that others, as well as the proprietors, may have occasion to go upon the island. To such, the bridge is an accommodation. Whether so many are thus accom- modated that it may be said to be of common convenience, *is a question which it was the province of the Legislature to de- termine,* and which may be presumed to have been correctly determined. We can therefore see no valid objection to the constitutionality of this grant."

In *Spring* vs. *Russell* (7 Maine, 229), the ques- tion was whether an Act of the Legislature cre- ating a corporation, and authorizing it to turn the course of a public navigable stream, and to take private property for that purpose. was constitutional. The Constitution of the State contained this clause: " Whenever the *public exigencies* require that the property of any individual shall be appropriated to public use, he shall receive a reasonable compensation therefor." The Court said:

"Under the above-mentioned limitations, it is the unquestioned province of the Legislature to determine as to the wisdom and expediency of a law, *and how far the public interest is concerned* (if in any degree), *and may properly be influential in the enactment of a law directly operating on private property.* * * * We apprehend that the question of constitutionality does not, *in judicial consideration,* depend on the *proportion* which the *public* interest bears to *private* interest, in the application of the restrictive principle on which the plaintiff's counsel relies."

In the case of the *Boston Water-Power Co.* vs. *Boston and Worcester Railroad Corporation* (23 Pick. 394), it was held that the necessity for a railroad in a given locality was a legislative question.

Said Chancellor Walworth, in *Beekman* vs. *The Saratoga and Schenectady Railroad Company* (3 Paige, 73):

" If the public interest can be in any way promoted by the taking of private property, *it must rest with the wisdom of the Legislature* to determine whether the benefit to the public will be of sufficient importance to render it expedient for them to exercise the right of eminent domain."

To the same effect is the opinion of Chief Justice Nelson, in *Taylor* vs. *Porter* (4 Hill, 151).

Van Horne vs. *Dorance,* 2 Dallas, 312.

Dunn vs. *The City Council,* Hrp. Rep. 189.

De Varaigne vs. *Fox,* 2 Blatchford, 95.

Charles River Bridge vs. *Warren River Bridge,* 7 Pick. 453.

The doctrine of this Court is to the same effect.

In the case of *Blanding* vs. *Burr,* 13 Cal. 350, Chief Justice Field said:

"There is no restriction as to the amount of the tax which may be imposed, *or the purpose to which the money received shall be applied.* The security against the abuse of the power of the Legislature is to be found in the wisdom and sense of justice of its members, and their relation to their constituents. It can impose a general tax upon all the property of the State, or a local tax upon the property of particular political subdivisions, as counties, cities and towns. The cases in which its power shall be exercised, and the extent to which the taxation in a particular instance shall be carried, *are matters exclusively within its own judgment,* subject to the qualifications of equality and uniformity in the assessment. * * * It may appropriate them (moneys raised by taxation) to claims which have no legal obligation, and are founded only in justice. Of the propriety of the appropriation, *as of the expediency of the taxation,* IT IS THE SOLE JUDGE. With the exercise of the power in *either* case, the *judiciary cannot interfere.*"

This case was followed in the case of the *Napa Valley Railroad Company* vs. *Napa County,* 30 Cal. 438.

In the case of *Beals* vs. *Amador County*, 35 Cal. 638, Justice Sprague said:

"The legislative department of our State Government is not, like the Congress of the United States, restricted in its sphere of action by a fixed chart of delegated powers. Its power represents the independent sovereignty of the people of the State, and is *supreme* and unlimited in all legitimate subject matters of legislation, and controlled only by such restrictions as are imposed by the organic law of the State.

"The *only restriction* imposed upon legislative discretion in the matter of taxation by our Constitution is, that it shall be equal and uniform, and in proportion to the value of the property taxed ; and this, it will be observed, is not a restriction of the *absolute* power to impose taxation, but simply a restriction upon the *mode* of its exercise. There being, then, no constitutional check or limitation of the legislative power to impose the tax, it would seem to follow necessarily that if the mode of its exercise, as provided by the Act, conforms to and is not in conflict with the constitutional restriction, the law is binding and obligatory, *and beyond the control of the judicial department of the State Government.*"

Here the whole scope and extent of the power of the judiciary over the subject of taxation is clearly stated. The courts may review the Acts of the Legislature so far as to determine whether the tax has been, or is to be, assessed equally and uniformly, and in proportion to the value of the property taxed. Beyond that the judicial department has no control, and the power of the Legislature is *absolute.* The soundness of this view cannot be impeached, and it leaves the object for which the power of taxation may be exercised, where it ought to be, wholly within the judgment and discretion of the Legislature, with no power of review in the courts.

In the case of the *People* vs. *San Francisco*, 36 Cal. 601, Justice Crockett said:

"It is not our province to discuss the *expediency or wisdom* of a Legislative Act. Our sole duty is, by applying just rules of construction to ascertain the true intent of the Legislature, *and carry it into effect.* If the Act is *unwise* or *oppressive* in its provisions, the fault is with the Legislature, *and we have no power to remedy the grievance.*"

In the case of *Sherman* vs. *Buick*, 32 Cal. 253 this Court has said:

"Whether a given road will subserve the public need or convenience is a question for the Government alone to determine. *The courts have nothing to do with it.* * *
* The ultimate decision of the question, whether a given road will subserve the public need or convenience, must rest somewhere, and it is wisely left for the Legislature to determine in such manner as they may provide."

To hold otherwise would be to place political power in the hands of the judiciary, and strip our system of Government of its popular form. To hold otherwise would be to hold that this Court, consisting of five persons only, is better informed as to the wants and necessities of the public than the one hundred and twenty who compose the legislative department, and may therefore override the judgment of that body on all questions

7

affecting the interests of the public. Upon all questions affecting the purposes and objects for which the powers of eminent domain and taxation may, or shall be exercised, the judgment of the law-making power is and ought to be conclusive. The arguments which have been made in this case would have been more appropriate if they had been made before the Legislature, for the Halls of Legislation, and not the Halls of Justice are the proper places to discuss what are public wants and necessities—what are public exigencies, and what are public uses. There the power to provide for them is lodged; and, *ex necessitate rei*, the incidental power to adjudge what they are.

PRECEDENTS.

Having shown that the power of taxation is a power to take the property of the citizen for public use, and that a railroad is a public use, the conclusion is inevitable—whether the question be considered from a legislative or judicial stand-point—that the former may be exercised in behalf of the latter, which is the ultimate point to be established. But the further question remains as to how far the Courts have followed this argument and applied its conclusions to legislation of this character; for precedent as well as principle is to be considered in the discussion of legal

questions. They do not always agree, and, sometimes, on grounds of public policy, the former is
allowed to override the latter.

This legislation, so far as its mode of working
is concerned, has been of two kinds—first, authorizing counties and cities to take stock in railroads;
and second, to donate their bonds. The validity
of the first kind has been declared by the highest
Courts of twenty-one States, and also by the Supreme Court of the United States. (See McCon-
nell's briefs filed in this case.) Only three States,
Iowa, Wisconsin and Michigan, have declared
against its validity; and recently Iowa, upon a
sober second thought, has taken back the decla-
ration, leaving only two States who have repu-
diated this legislation, against twenty-two which
now sustain it. It may well be doubted if any
legal principle can be found in respect to which
such an unanimity of judicial opinion can be
shown. Of a question so situated, a rational conflict of authority cannot be affirmed.

Against the validity of donations there have
been, of a late date, four decisions: one in New
York, one in Iowa, one in Wisconsin, and one in
Michigan. The first is entitled to no consideration as a precedent, for it was not rendered by a
Court of last resort. The second, as just stated,
has since been overruled by the same Court.

This leaves two States, Wisconsin and Michigan, standing solitary and alone in opposition to this species of legislation. The Supreme Court of Wisconsin is composed of three Judges, one of whom dissented. The Supreme Court of Michigan is composed of four Judges, one of whom dissented. So the great industry of the Attorney-General and his coadjutors has found, in all the civilized world, only five Judges who have had the effrontery to outrage reason and precedent, by declaring this legislation unconstitutional. In the language of the Supreme Court of the United States, "they stand out in unenviable solitude and notoriety." Their decisions can be accounted for in no way unless it be that their judgments were warped by outside influences. It may be that the party whip was cracked over their heads by the Executive of the State—it may be that newspaper editors, who know a little of everything and not much of anything, dictated their judgments, or reminded them that those very profound jurists, the people, were expecting them to decide as they did. But be the cause what it may, their judgments are opposed. as I have attempted to show, to both principle and precedent. Yet Counsel upon the other side have gravely assured this Court, that the current of decisions, upon this subject, is turning. Counsel have mis-

taken a slight crevasse for the true channel, and
from that, the judicial waters,

"With the hollow roar
Of tides receding from th' insulted shore,"

have already commenced to disappear. True, like
the waters of the Mississippi when the Storm
King breathes upon them, they have broken
through their banks, under the pressure of popular clamor; but like them, when the storm has
passed, they are now returning to their old channel, *ubi currere solebat.* Iowa has commenced to fill
up the breach, and Wisconsin and Michigan may
yet join her, when the panic under which they
have been laboring shall have ceased.

No Distinction between Subscriptions and Donations.

The Courts of Wisconsin and Michigan have
not undertaken to distinguish between subscriptions and donations—have not held that
the former are valid and the latter not. They
have taken the broad ground that both are
equally outside of the taxing power. Yet fear-
ing, evidently, that this Court, in view of its
course heretofore in relation to subscriptions,
might hold them valid, on the ground of *stare decisis* if no other, counsel have endeavored to distinguish between them and donations—maintain-

ing that although the former may be valid, the latter may not. In this effort they are placed in the awkward position of assailing, in part, the only cases upon which they rely for support, in other respects, for as just stated those cases are not based, in any respect, upon any supposed distinction between subscriptions and donations. No Court, so far as I am advised, has held that subscriptions are valid and that donations are not. Such an attack upon their friends is calculated to weaken their cause, but be the consequence upon their own heads.

The argument in support of this alleged distinction is this: that in the case of a subscription a supposed equivalent is returned to the tax-payer in stock, whereas in the case of a donation he receives no return. Neither is true as stated. The tax-payer does not receive stock in return; the county or city, as the case may be, receives it, and the only benefit which the tax-payer receives from the transaction, is not an individual or several benefit, but a benefit which is common to himself and all the other members of the community. In the case of a donation, the tax-payer receives his share of the common benefit which flows from the construction of the road. The only difference, then, is in the amount of the common benefit returned. That there is this difference I admit. But a difference in the *quan-*

tum of benefit received, it is obvious cannot be made the test as to whether the power to do the act exists or not. There being a benefit in each case, differing only in degree, no distinction, on the score of power between the two can be maintained which is founded upon the question of benefit. The fact that the one results in a greater benefit than the other, is, therefore, a mere difference in *circumstance*, and not a distinction in *principle*. That no such distinction can be admitted must be apparent, when it is remembered that we are dealing with a question of *power* and not of contract—a power which is sovereign and which acts on the citizen not *by* his consent but *against* it.

The idea, which is one of the corner-stones upon which the opponents of this legislation build, that no money can be taken from the citizen by taxation for any purpose, or object, which will make no direct return of individual benefit, however captivating and plausible to the popular mind, is altogether deceptive. It is always true in theory, but so far as perception goes frequently false in fact. All taxes levied for the support of the public schools, and all charitable or eleemosynary institutions are illustrations. The taxpayer who has no children to educate is nevertheless taxed to pay for the education of his neighbors'! The tax-payer who has no use for hospitals, asylums or almshouses, and derives from neither a tangible individual benefit is nevertheless taxed for their support. That such an exercise of the taxing power is unconstitutional however, no one will pretend; yet it is, if the logic by which the invalidity of this legislation is sought to be maintained, is sound. But it is a mistake to suppose, even in such cases, that no benefit is realized. Though not in a certain sense perceptible, a tangible or common and, therefore, personal benefit is nevertheless received, in the general advancement of education, civilization, science, art, and everything else which constitutes an element in political, moral or social progress.

DECISIONS IN THIS STATE.

It is said, by the opponents of this legislation, that the decisions of this Court in relation to this subject are conflicting. I deny the proposition. The first case which had any bearing upon the question was *Lowe* vs. *The Mayor etc. of the City of Marysville* (5 Cal. 214.) The question presented was whether the city of Marysville could take stock in the "Citizens' Steam Navigation Company." There had been no Act passed by the Legislature, like those now being considered, authorizing the city to take stock in that, or any other company, and the existence of the power turned upon the construction of the following clause in the city charter:

" If the Common Council desire to take stock in any public improvement, or loan the credit of the city to any improvement, or effect a loan for any purpose, for a sum exceeding five thousand dollars, they shall submit a proposition for taking such stock, or effecting such loan, stating the amount of loan or stock, to the electors of the city of Marysville, at a special election to be held for that purpose, upon the Common Council giving twenty days published notice of the same; and if two-thirds of the electors vote in favor of such proposition, or propositions, the Common Council shall have power to effect such loan or take such stock—but not otherwise—and pledge the faith of the city for such loan or stock."

In respect to this statute two points were presented by counsel for the decision of the Court:

First—Whether it was intended by this statute to authorize the city to take stock in or to loan its credit to other than such public improvements as are of a strictly municipal character—such as water works, gas works, alms houses, hospitals, etc.

Second—If it did, whether it was not unconstitutional.

8

The Court held that it was the intention of the statute to authorize the city to take stock in or loan its credit only to such public improvements as were of a strictly municipal character—that is to say, such improvements as are indispensable to the wants of the city, such as water works, gas works, etc.

Having come to this conclusion, it is obvious there was no occasion to consider the second point, yet this Court took it up and decided in effect, that if there had been, which there was not, any law authorizing the city to take stock in the "Citizens' Steam Navigation Company," it would have been unconstitutional. It is not necessary to say that a question decided under such circumstances is not decided at all, and the decision is of no force, *as such*, and can only be referred to for what it may be worth as an argument, not as a precedent which is binding upon this Court. So we find that in the next case which came before the Court, which was the case of a special statute authorizing the county of Yuba to take stock in a railroad, this case, although cited by counsel as an authority against the constitutionality of the latter Act, is not even referred to in the opinion of the Court. (*Pattison* vs. *Board of Supervisors of Yuba County*, 13 Cal., 175.)

The question now being considered came before the Court for the first time in the case last cited. It was directly involved in that case and the decision was directly in favor of the constitutionality of this character of legislation, so far as it relates to subscriptions. From that time to the present the rule has never been departed from. When in 1864, the Court was reorganized under the amendments to the Constitution which took effect at the commencement of last year, the Judges who then came upon the bench found that their predecessors had declared such legislation to be constitutional, and that upon the faith of that decision large amounts of city and county bonds had been issued, and that to overturn the rule of their predecessors, whether it did or did not meet with their approval, would be to disregard the doctrine of *stare decisis* in a case where every consideration required its application. They accordingly followed the rule adopted by their predecessors as they ought to have done. Yet for this discharge of what was obviously their judicial duty, they have been accused of yielding to outside influence by a gentleman now holding a prominent position in the government of the State, who has found in the circumstance that they did not overturn a rule which had become the sole foundation of large pecuniary interests, cause to congratulate the

country because four of their number have re-
tired from the Bench. This gentleman, then, *as
counsel*, advocated the same doctrine which the
Attorney General now advocates. Is his evident
hostility to those gentlemen due in any measure
to the fact that his logic and eloquence failed to
convert them to his faith? Did his eyes upon this
subject become so jaundiced while he occupied
the position of counsel that they are still dis-
eased upon this question? Be that as it may, it
is not out of place for me, who knew them so in-
timately in all their judicial relations, to say, of
three of them, that though they were neither of
them deacons of a church, yet were they in all
the qualities of an honest man the full peers of
their assailant, and in all the characteristics of a
lawyer they were his superiors, for they considered it to be their duty as Judges to read the
Constitution and the laws as they had been written, and not as they might conceive they ought
to have been written.

This Court has never had occasion to pass upon
the constitutionality of laws authorizing counties
and cities to aid in the construction of railroads
by donations, so-called, and the question whether
any distinction can be made on the score of principle between donations and subscriptions is
therefore open.

Stare Decisis.

There is one other legal principle to which reference must be made, before all the points will have been touched upon, which are involved in this discussion. The principle to which I refer is *stare decisis*; or the rule by which all Courts are governed in respect to their previous decisions. For obvious reasons, uniformity of ruling upon the same question, on the part of the Courts, is demanded upon grounds of public policy. This rule applies with binding force to all questions affecting the rights of property. Were Courts to overrule themselves upon questions of that character, there would be no security for property— men could never invest their money with any certainty that they would be allowed to enjoy the benefit or advantage to be derived from their investment. Hence in such cases, although the Courts may become satisfied, that a wiser and better rule might have been adopted in the first instance, yet they adhere to it, because a departure from it would retroact and unsettle the rights of property acquired under the previous ruling. The present subject affords an apt illustration of this principle. It is estimated that more than three millions of county and city bonds have been issued and have been bought as an investment by private parties, on the strength of the decisions of this Court, that the laws under which they were issued were constitutional. Were this Court now to adopt a contrary rule, all these bonds would become as worthless as the paper upon which they are printed. Consequences like this must have, as they ought to have, a controlling weight with the Courts, and they have steadily refused in all such cases to disturb their previous decisions. A change in the Constitution, or the law, as the case may be, is followed by no such mischievous consequences, and the latter is therefore declared to be the only remedy.

––––––––––

The Wisconsin and Michigan Cases.

It may be thought that some more direct notice, should be given to the recent decisions in Wisconsin and Michigan. But it is sufficient to say that they are but two against twenty-three, and are therefore entitled to no consideration as precedents. So far as they represent a principle, they are opposed to my position, and in fortifying that I have necessarily undertaken to expose their fallacies. The vice, in those cases, lies in the fact that they proceed upon the theory that railroads are private *enterprises*, and not public improvements, and therefore that they cannot be constitutionally aided by taxation. That this theory is wrong, that it is contradicted by reason

and an overwhelming array of legislative and judicial authorities I have attempted to show. In my
judgment those Courts, in their zeal to prevent
what they conceived to be unwise legislation, mis-
took expediency for principle, and founded their
judgment on the former and not upon the latter,
forgetting that questions of policy are for the
Legislature and not the Judiciary, and that the
latter can never be held responsible for the unwise acts of the former. Judges are but men, and
like other men are liable to err. I have never
been able to discover any substantial difference
between a good lawyer on the bench and a good
lawyer off the bench, except that the former is
able, by reason of his position, to tell you what
the law is, while the latter, by reason of his position, can only tell you what he thinks it is. Nor
should we be surprised to sometimes find them
wrong, and when we do, or think we do, we
should not hasten to account for their supposed
error by charging them with a dishonest purpose,
or seek a reversal of their decisions by popular
clamor, or by notifying them, in advance of their
decision, that if they do not decide in a particular
way, the legal profession, as well as those eminent
jurists, the people at large, will be thrown off
their balance with astonishment and surprise. It
is unreasonable to suppose that judges can escape
error, when we remember that even those filling

other responsible positions — men of supposed learning and ability, are sometimes seized with an insane desire to startle the world with the announcement of some hitherto undiscovered truth, or become so blinded by an unsuccessful opposition to the progress of civil liberty, that they are ready and willing, in season and out of season, to maintain that "the Federal Constitution can be amended, but cannot be changed," or that " Negroes are entitled to vote but cannot be allowed to exercise the right, until Congress has passed a law, by which every person who undertakes to prevent it, can be sent to the penitentiary."

My conclusion is that railroads are public highways, and as such may be aided and fostered by the Legislature. at the public expense, through the the exercise of the taxing power.

S. W. SANDERSON,

For the S. P. R. R. Co.

www.ingramcontent.com/pod-product-compliance
Lightning Source LLC
Chambersburg PA
CBHW021628270326
41931CB00008B/927